To Dr. Jim,
Congratulations and Best
Wishes.   Love
Norma + Roger Griest
5/31/87

HIGH ABOVE THE HOLY LAND

Library of Congress Cataloging
in Publication Data applied for

ISBN 0-8307-1153-8

Designed and produced by
Three's Company
12 Flitcroft Street
London WC2H 8DJ

Photographs © 1986 Sonia
Halliday and Laura Lushington
using Pentax 6×7 equipment.

Scripture quotations in this
publication are from the Holy
Bible, New International
Version.
Copyright © 1973, 1978,
1984 by International Bible
Society. Published by Hodder
and Stoughton.

Worldwide co-edition
organized and produced by
Angus Hudson Ltd,
Greater London House,
Hampstead Road, London
NW1 7QX.

All aerial photographs by Sonia
Halliday and Laura Lushington.
All inset photographs by Sonia
Halliday and Laura Lushington,
except p. 26 (Barbara Warley),
p. 46 (Barry Searle), and p. 52
(Jane Taylor).

Maps and diagrams by
James Macdonald.

Design: Peter Wyart MSIAD

Printed in Great Britain by
Purnell Book Production Ltd
Paulton, Bristol

HIGH ABOVE THE HOLY LAND

UNIQUE AERIAL PHOTOGRAPHS OF ISRAEL
BY SONIA HALLIDAY AND LAURA LUSHINGTON

TEXT BY TIM DOWLEY

Regal Books
A Division of GL Publications
Ventura, California, U.S.A.

ISRAEL

Reference map showing location of places illustrated in the book; figures refer to the appropriate pages.

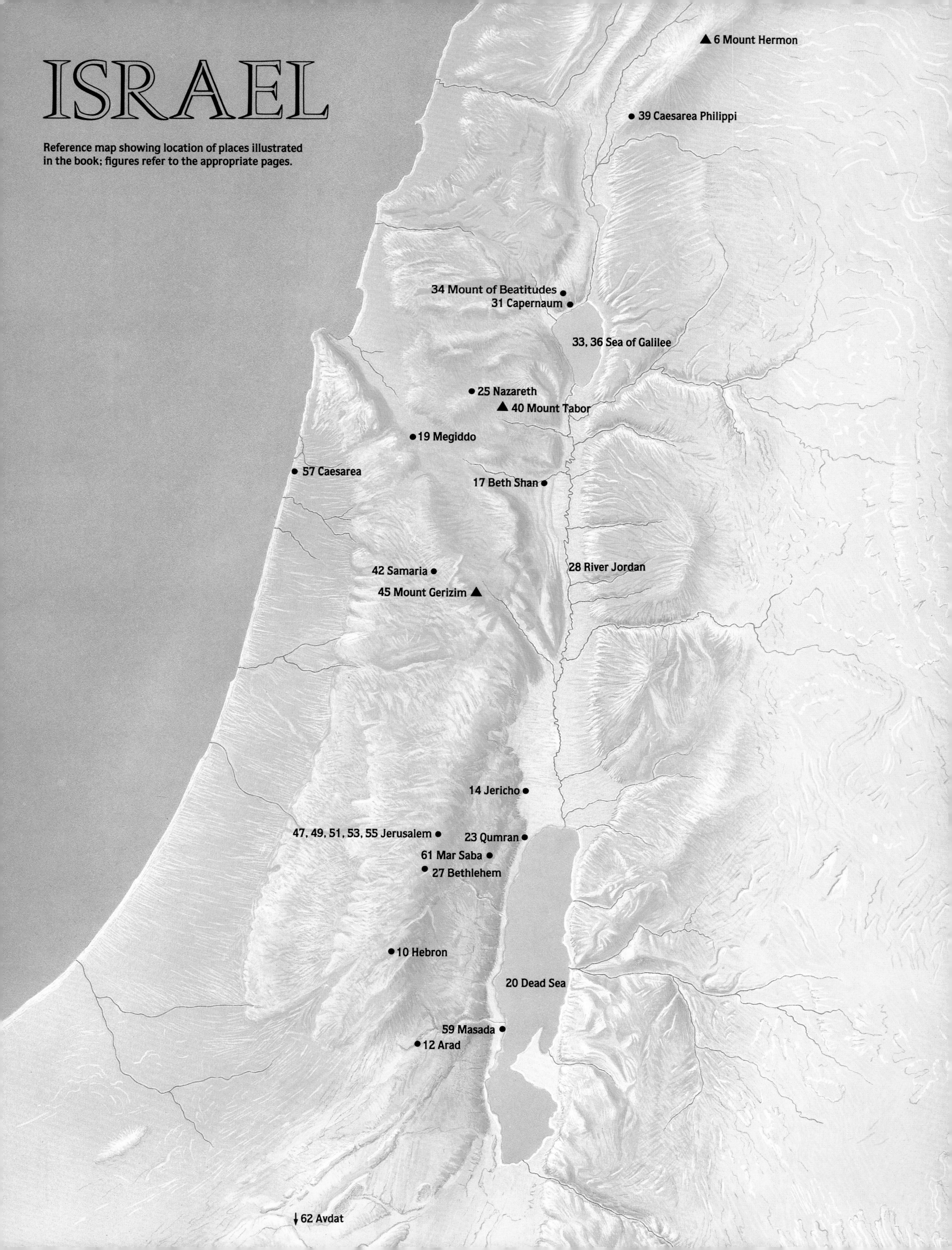

▲ 6 Mount Hermon

● 39 Caesarea Philippi

34 Mount of Beatitudes ●
31 Capernaum ●

33, 36 Sea of Galilee

● 25 Nazareth
▲ 40 Mount Tabor

● 19 Megiddo

● 57 Caesarea

17 Beth Shan ●

42 Samaria ●

28 River Jordan

45 Mount Gerizim ▲

14 Jericho ●

47, 49, 51, 53, 55 Jerusalem ●   23 Qumran ●

61 Mar Saba ●
● 27 Bethlehem

● 10 Hebron

20 Dead Sea

59 Masada ●
● 12 Arad

↓ 62 Avdat

CONTENTS

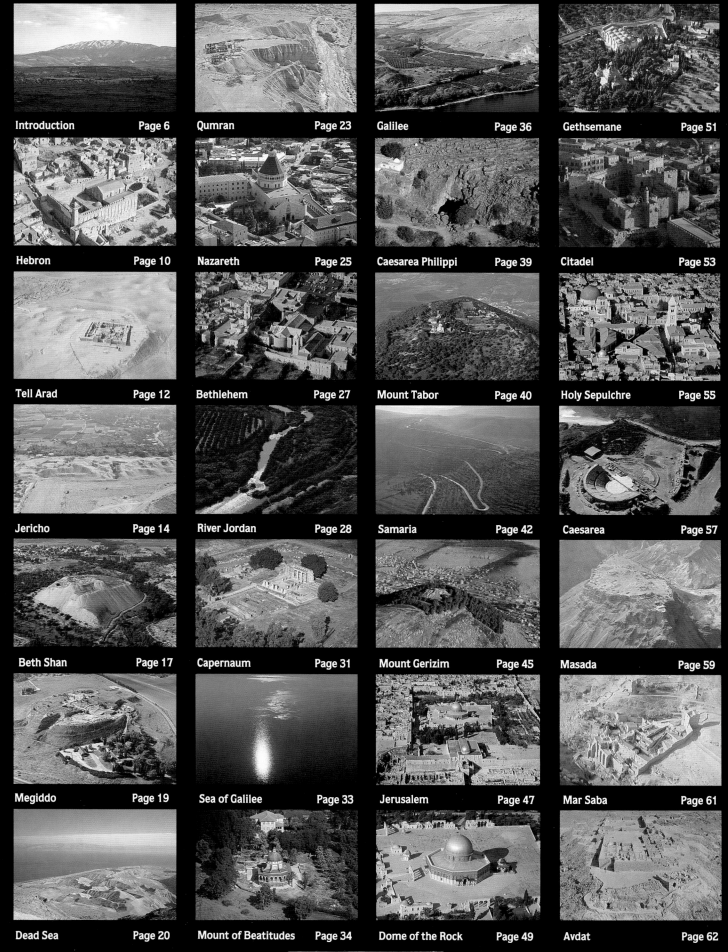

Introduction

Most people who visit the Holy Land today are taken from one place to another by motor coach, along modern roads. But others, who have the necessary time and interest, prefer to travel through it on foot, not by today's motorways but by older paths. Thus they enter more directly into the experience of ancient travellers, and by covering the country on the ground they gain a knowledge of it which is denied to the traveller by coach.

There is, however, a very modern way of seeing the land as a whole: that is, from the air. Aerial survey cannot take the place of exploration on the ground, but it has the great advantage of enabling one to take the country in at a glance – to 'view the landscape o'er', much as Moses did when from Mount Pisgah he saw as far as Dan in the north, the Negev in the south, and 'all the land of Judah as far as the western sea' (Deuteronomy 34: 2,3).

Something of the advantage of viewing the land from the air can be derived from a study of aerial photographs, like those presented here in *High Above the Holy Land*.

If, looking towards the north, we survey the Holy Land from west to east, we can distinguish parallel bands of territory running north and south—four west of the Jordan and another to the east. The most westerly is the Mediterranean coastal plain, starting from the point at the southern end of the Bay of Haifa where Mount Carmel runs into the sea, and stretching south towards the Egyptian frontier. Next we have the lowlands, the

Mount Hermon, which feeds the river Dan with its snows.

Shephelah, with gently sloping hills and wide east-west valleys, forming a transition between the coastal plain and the central mountain ridge. This ridge, the third of the parallel bands, consists of a succession of hills rising to heights of over 3,000 feet (900 metres); it starts in Upper Galilee and continues south to the Negev.

East of the central ridge is the Jordan valley, part of the Great Rift Valley which stretches south to the Red Sea and East Africa. This major geological fault is well below Mediterranean sea level: at the Sea of Galilee (Lake Tiberias) it is nearly 700 feet (200 metres) below, and it descends rapidly until, at the surface of the Dead Sea, it is about 1,300 feet (400 metres) below – the lowest area on the face of the earth – while the bottom of the sea is as deep again. In the words of George Adam Smith, 'there may be something on the surface of another planet to match the Jordan Valley: there is nothing on this'. South of the Dead Sea the rift valley continues as the Arabah until it reaches the Gulf of Aqaba.

To the east of the Jordan valley rise the TransJordanian hills; between them and the Euphrates-Tigris valley lies the Syrian Desert.

The hill country of Upper Galilee is separated from Mount Gilboa and the hills of Samaria, in the centre of the country, by the fertile Plain of Jezreel (Lower Galilee). The main route from Mesopotamia and Syria to Egypt – 'the way of the sea' (Isaiah 9:1) – came from the north through Damascus; it crossed the Jordan by several

The impressive archaeological excavations at Hazor are clearly visible from the air.

branches both north and south of the Sea of Galilee and turned west through the Plain of Jezreel, crossed the mountain ridge by the pass of Megiddo and then ran south along the coastal plain.

Another ancient road ran from north to south through TransJordan to Aqaba: it is mentioned in Numbers 20:17 as 'the king's highway'. It has in more recent times been part of the pilgrim way from Damascus to Mecca, and to this day the main north-south thoroughfare through the kingdom of Jordan follows essentially the same line.

These natural features, and the roads whose course was adapted to them, did much to determine the way in which the history of the Holy Land and its inhabitants unfolded itself.

Nazareth in Galilee, where Jesus was brought up, was a place of no great importance, but from the high ground above it one could look down on many scenes which figured in the history of Israel. The Plain of Jezreel, to the south, had witnessed a succession of decisive battles, such as Barak's victory over Sisera at the river Kishon and good King Josiah's fatal defeat by the Egyptian king at Megiddo, at the western end of the plain. To the east Mount Tabor rose from the plain to a height of over 1,900 feet (588 metres). It was here that Barak mustered his forces to take the field against Sisera; it was on its summit, according to later but doubtful tradition, that the transfiguration of Jesus took place. South of the Plain of Jezreel, slightly to the left, was Mount Gilboa, where King Saul fell in battle against the Philistines. No intelligent child brought up in Nazareth could have failed to gain an acquaintance with the nation's early history.

The road from the Sea of Galilee to Acco, on the Mediterranean coast north of the Gulf of Haifa, ran a few miles to the north of Nazareth, while the Way of the Sea ran not far to the south. Along these roads, especially the latter, trading caravans and military convoys travelled in both directions.

Some four miles north-west of Nazareth stood the fortified city of Sepphoris, where Herod Antipas, tetrarch of Galilee, had his court for the first twenty-five years of Jesus' life, until he moved it to his new city of Tiberias, west of the lake, about the year 22. Rumours of incidents at Herod's court in Sepphoris would quickly reach Nazareth, and may have provided some of the illustrative detail in those parables of Jesus where kings and great persons figure.

Herod Antipas was the youngest son of Herod the Great, king of the Jews, whose reign over the whole of Palestine was coming to an end at the time of Jesus' birth. Herod owed his throne to the Roman state, and when he died the emperor decided to partition his kingdom among three of his sons. Herod Antipas received Galilee and Peraea (southern TransJordan), Philip received a tetrarchy east and north-east of the Sea of Galilee (with its capital at Caesarea Philippi, near one of the sources of the Jordan), while Archelaus (mentioned in Matthew 2:22) received Judea and Samaria. Archelaus' subjects found his rule so oppressive that they petitioned the Roman emperor for his removal, and in AD 6 Judea (with Samaria) became a Roman province, administered by a governor appointed by the emperor. The best known of these governors is Pontius Pilate (whose term of office lasted from 26 to 36); other governors mentioned in the New Testament are Felix (52–59) and Festus (59–62).

The Roman theatre, Caesarea.

When danger threatened from Herod Antipas, it was easy for Jesus and his disciples to take a boat across the lake into the territory of Philip. When Jesus visited Judea and Jerusalem, he found himself in territory directly ruled by Rome, where the question of paying tribute to Caesar was a burning political issue, as it was not in Galilee. It was by a Roman judge that he was sentenced to death, and it was by the Roman method of crucifixion that the sentence was executed.

When we take account in this way of the geographical and historical setting, we appreciate better that the men and women who appear in the Bible story were real human beings of flesh and blood, and the events recorded there actually took place in the places and at the times indicated. Some of those men and women lived all their lives in the same place, but many of them travelled widely, keeping constantly on the move. When we picture them in their various real-life contexts, we begin to understand more clearly much that is recorded about them.

Many features of the Holy Land have changed since Bible days. The bedouin tents in the wilderness of Judea may still look much as they did in Abraham's time, but the people who live in them keep in touch with the outside world by means of transistor radios. Yet we can still see the difference between the wilderness – that is, the pasture-land for sheep and goats – where they have their home and the cultivated land which adjoins it; we can appreciate the difference between the nomad's way of life and that of the farmer, just as we can appreciate the difference between country life and city life. When the Israelites were about to enter the Holy Land after their servitude in Egypt, Moses told them of the change they would find from the irrigation methods with which they were familiar in Egypt, by which the flood-water of the Nile was carefully channelled to every field and garden. 'But the land you are crossing the Jordan to take possession of is a land of mountains and valleys that drinks rain from heaven' (Deuteronomy 11: 11,12). That difference persists today: Egypt's fertility still depends on the Nile, even if the river is now dammed at Aswan, and the Holy Land still depends on seasonal rainfall for the regular production of the fruits of the earth.

Today, as in Bible days, human life is largely controlled by natural conditions. To learn something of those conditions, therefore, helps us to view the lives and actions of Bible characters from a proper perspective. Whether the places mentioned in the Bible are still busy centres of human activity, or have been covered over for centuries and now, thanks to excavation, stand as monuments to a by-gone way of life, they can teach us much about the people and events associated with them.

The realism of the Bible, and of its geographical information, is constantly being proved in the Holy Land. Archaeologists know where to excavate to unearth ancient sites, because the Bible indicates their location. Mineralogists find hints in the Bible which lead them to mineral deposits. The guidance it affords about the existence of springs of water is of great value in the development of the land. While the equipment of Joshua and other military leaders of Bible times has long since been superseded, their strategy and tactics, based on a careful appraisal of the terrain, are by no means out of date, as strategists and tacticians have proved in the twentieth century.

Field Marshal Allenby, who conquered Palestine from the Turks in 1917–18, acknowledged his indebtedness in the planning of his campaign to a once well-known geographical commentary on the biblical narrative, George Adam Smith's *Historical Geography of the Holy Land*. (Although the last edition of this work was published in 1931, it remains of great value.)

The Holy Land is the setting of by far the greater part of the biblical narrative. That narrative tells how Abraham and his family came from the east and led a nomad existence as pastoralists in the Holy Land, and how, after his family had gone to Egypt in a time of famine and been drafted into forced labour gangs there, they were liberated under the leadership of Moses and brought by his successor, Joshua, into the Holy Land to occupy their settlements there. It tells how David, their king, was able to unify the nation and establish a brief supremacy for it over the surrounding states. It tells further how, when national prosperity dwindled and independence itself was lost, the hope that the God of Israel would fulfil his promises to his people was kept alive by the prophets and found its fulfilment at last in the coming of Jesus.

This long story, extending over nearly 2,000 years, is not set in a vacuum. It interacts with the story of great world-empires: Egypt, Assyria, Babylon, Persia, Macedonia, Rome. If the record of those empires helps to illuminate the biblical narrative, the biblical narrative also makes its distinctive contribution to the record of those empires. Here is real life – real life not only in the setting of the distant past, but real life for men and women today.

F. F. Bruce

Taking the photographs

We first thought of photographing Israel from the air when we found that we were unable effectively to photograph the magnificent gorge and fortifications of Mar Saba from the ground, and also that, as women, we were not allowed through the gates of this Greek Orthodox monastery.

We discovered an excellent pilot, Moni Haramati, who flies helicopters in the Israeli army. He went through the list of sites we had selected, organized a flight plan and submitted it to the military authorities. Our flight schedule was very tight; we had to be in and out of particular zones by set times because of military manoeuvres. Flying over the Judean desert, its undulating hills and wadis looking like a relief map, two patrolling fighter-planes suddenly streaked beneath us – a beautiful sight, but strictly not to be photographed. Naturally, all our film had to be censored by the military, although in the event only two frames had to be cut; a radio station had strayed into our viewfinder without our knowledge!

Our aircraft, a Cessna 172 with its door removed, proved to be very versatile. We used three 6 × 7 Pentax cameras hung on a safety wire locked around our waists and around the seat. (Apparently another photographer

The photographers, Sonia Halliday and Laura Lushington.

The Temple Mount, Jerusalem, from the air, with Mount Scopus in the background.

had almost hanged himself by having the cameras round his neck!) Our method allowed the second photographer to load and unload the cameras without any danger of dropping them out of the plane.

We used 105mm and 300mm lenses – the latter proving best for accurate light readings. With the 300mm lens, the Dome of the Rock almost filled the viewfinder from a height of 500 feet (150 metres). Much to other photographers' surprise, we used Ektachrome Professional EPN 120 (100 ASA) rather than 400 ASA, which gives a blue cast, especially in aerial photography. We found that with 100 ASA the colour reproduction was excellent, shooting at 1/1000 second at f/4 or f/5.6, depending on the colour density of the land below.

The itinerary

Israel is a tiny country, only 260 miles (420 kilometres) from north to south. Even so, it took us more than ten hours flying time to cover the major sites. It was a long leg down to Avdat in the Negev, 40 miles (64 kilometres) due south of Beersheba, but well worth it for the aerial view of the Byzantine castle and the two churches, built on the foundations of Nabataean and Roman temples. Also clearly visible from the air was the ancient winepress.

Flying north from Avdat to Beersheba, we looked for the black goat-hair tents of the bedouin, which these days all too often have been replaced with shiny corrugated-iron shacks! It is extremely difficult to find a photogenic encampment that doesn't have its prominent 50-gallon oil drum or brightly-coloured plastic bucket. From the air, the bedouin sheep, feeding in circles, looked like so many tiny maggots.

Our prime object was to obtain aerial photographs of sites of biblical interest. Masada was the most rewarding, since it is possible to fly within 100 feet (30 metres) of Herod's summer palace, perched on the northern tip of this massive natural rock fortress. Also clearly visible are the Roman military encampments south and west of the ancient stronghold.

We then flew to the far north of Israel, to Baniyas – biblical Caesarea Philippi – one of the sources of the river Jordan. This provided our only heart-stopping experience, as we flew straight in towards the vertical cliff. Our pilot, Mani, was trying to manoeuvre into the perfect position for photography, and was clearly waiting for us to say 'OK – we've got it! We swerved away only just in time – afterwards neither of us dared think just how close we'd been to the cliff!

Mount Hermon, north-east of Baniyas, shows many different faces, many moods. We have seen it covered by snow and draped in heavy rain-clouds; but this time it was not at all dramatic and, sadly, un-photogenic. From

Baniyas we followed the river Jordan south to the Sea of Galilee, passing on our way fish-ponds and acres of banana plantations and citrus groves. We could see clearly cattle grazing on the green scrubland flats that divide the Jordan into several tributaries as it meanders down the Bethsaida valley into the Sea of Galilee.

We were looking forward to photographing the octagonal building at Capernaum which represents the remains of a fifth-century church built over the supposed house of the apostle Peter. We had thought this would be the ideal way of showing its unusual shape – but it was not to be! In the two weeks since our last visit to Capernaum, the archaeologists had roofed the area over with shining corrugated iron.

Turbulence

Flying over the Sea of Galilee, we encountered considerable turbulence. It was certainly not conducive to photography – though we were both relieved that we were being thrown around in the air rather than in a small fishing boat on the sea below, where it is commonplace for a storm to blow up in a matter of minutes.

Mount Tabor, which rises to over 1900 feet (588 metres) above the Jezreel valley, is similarly seen to the best advantage from the air. Ruins of the earlier church at the east end of the present Franciscan basilica can be seen clearly. From Tabor we flew to Megiddo, but by this time it was mid-morning, and the famous site was over-run with visitors. After five or six circuits, we managed to get some shots without too many of them in sight!

We landed at Haifa to re-fuel both the plane and ourselves. Then, after a quick look at Acco (ancient Acre), we flew southwards down the Mediterranean coast to Caesarea. The first remains we spotted there were the two Roman aqueducts running north-south, parallel to the sea, and then the ancient harbour, with Roman columns lying half-submerged in the deep blue-green water. The Roman theatre stands out prominently from every angle, and it is still easy to imagine Caesarea as a thriving Roman port.

Because of commercial air traffic, we had to fly south of Tel-Aviv before turning inland and flying east to Jerusalem. En route we passed over Latrun monastery, near one of the two possible sites of biblical Emmaus. Climbing steadily most of the way – Jerusalem is over 2600 feet (800 metres) above sea-level – we had a superb view of the walls of the Holy City in the afternoon light.

To complete our aerial photography of the Holy Land we made a short detour (Jerusalem airport is about twelve miles (twenty kilometres) north of the city centre) and took shots of the Old City and the Mount of Olives, with the Judean hills and the Dead Sea beyond. Jerusalem, the city that holds a magnetic attraction for everyone who is fortunate enough to visit.

We should like to thank Yacov Margolin and Lee Silvermann of El Al Airlines for flying our team out to Israel, together with our equipment, which weighed close on 200 kilos. Our thanks also to Maurice Kushelevitch for the very high standard of film-processing which enabled us to see results within two hours. We are also constantly grateful to John Raddon of Pentax (UK) Ltd, who has helped and advised us with our Pentax 6 × 7 equipment over the years. Our especial thanks to Edward St Maur FBIPP, FRSA, FRPS, of Chepstow and Bath, for all his invaluable advice and help about aerial photography.

Sonia Halliday
Laura Lushington

Hebron

'Ephron the Hittite was sitting among his people and he replied to Abraham in the hearing of all the Hittites who had come to the gate of his city. "No, my lord," he said. "Listen to me; I give you the field, and I give you the cave that is in it. I give it to you in the presence of my people. Bury your dead."

'... So Ephron's field in Machpelah near Mamre — both the field and the cave in it, and all the trees within the borders of the field — was legally made over to Abraham as his property in the presence of all the Hittites who had come to the gate of the city. Afterwards Abraham buried his wife Sarah in the cave in the field of Machpelah near Mamre (which is at Hebron) in the land of Canaan. So the field and the cave in it were legally made over to Abraham by the Hittites as a burial site.'
Genesis 23:10,11,17–20

Hebron is one of the world's oldest cities, and has been continuously occupied from its earliest period, when it was settled by the Canaanites.

Hebron's significance in biblical history begins when Abraham camped nearby at the oaks of Mamre, where he built an altar to the Lord (Genesis 13:18). It was while he was still at Mamre that the Lord appeared to Abraham, promising him a son (Genesis 18). However, the only land that Abraham owned was what he obtained from Ephron as a burial place for his wife Sarah. Later Abraham himself, his son Isaac, his daughter-in-law Rebekah, his grandson Jacob and Jacob's wife Leah were all buried here too.

When the Israelites later came to conquer Canaan, Hebron was given to the valiant Caleb and his descendants (Joshua 14). Hebron again achieved prominence when the young King David succeeded King Saul. For the first seven years of his reign Hebron served as his capital city, and it was here that the elders of Israel anointed him king; later David transferred his capital to Jerusalem.

Herod the Great constructed the massive edifice which still stands over the Cave of Machpelah (**aerial photograph**). The masonry of the great outer walls is distinctively Herodian, and similar in appearance to the Herodian remains in the platform on which the Dome of the Rock in Jerusalem now stands. In the sixth century the Emperor Justinian built a church over the Cave of Machpelah, inside the Herodian enclosure, but this was converted into a mosque when the Muslims successfully invaded. The building is known today as Haram El-Khalil, or Shrine of the Friend, since the Muslims see Abraham as the friend of God (**inset**). It was the Muslims who added the minarets to the outer walls. Inside the courtyard are monuments to the patriarchs — Abraham, Sarah, Jacob and Leah; inside the mosque itself are two more monuments — to Isaac and Rebekah.

Tell Arad

This impressive and important archaeological site lies west of the Dead Sea and east of the city of Beersheba. It was excavated between 1962 and 1967 by the Israeli archaeologists Y. Aharoni and Ruth Amiran, who discovered two major sets of remains: a Canaanite city dating from the Bronze Age, before the Israelites conquered the land, and a citadel, which was occupied from the twelfth or eleventh century BC to the second century BC.

When the Israelites attempted to enter the Promised Land from the south, they were driven back by the king of Arad:

'When the Canaanite king of Arad, who lived in the Negev, heard that Israel was coming along the road to Atharim, he attacked the Israelites and captured some of them. Then Israel made this vow to the LORD: "If you will deliver these people into our hands, we will totally destroy their cities." The LORD listened to Israel's plea and gave the Canaanites over to them. They completely destroyed them and their towns; so the place was named Hormah.'
Numbers 21:1–3

When Joshua finally took the city, it was given to the tribe of Judah.

It is believed that it was during the reign of King Solomon that the city was developed further and its fortifications strengthened. The Iron Age citadel which dates from this period can be seen in the foreground of the aerial photograph; in the distance are the remains of the earlier Canaanite city.

Within the walls of the citadel have been discovered the remains of a temple whose structure seems to have been similar to what we know of the first temple at Jerusalem, as we understand it from the account given in 1 Kings 6. The Arad temple is the only Jewish religious building of its type so far to have been excavated. Archaeological excavation is not allowed within the boundaries of the Temple Mount in Jerusalem, so the information available from Arad is of great value in understanding Jewish religious architecture. Like the Jerusalem temple, the Arad temple was situated within a broad courtyard, with an altar at its centre. Like the Jerusalem temple, too, the Arad temple seems to have had a pillar on each side of its entrance.

In 920 BC, soon after its construction, the citadel was captured by the Pharaoh Sheshonk, known in the Old Testament as Shishak. But Arad was soon recaptured by Judah, which retained it until it fell to the Babylonian invaders in 586 BC.

Inset: A bedouin encampment in the Negev.

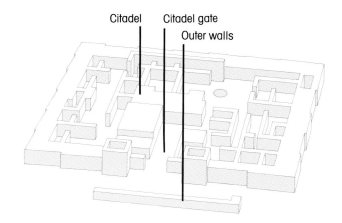

Citadel   Citadel gate
                Outer walls

Jericho

'Now Jericho was tightly shut up because of the Israelites. No-one went out and no-one came in. Then the LORD said to Joshua, "See, I have delivered Jericho into your hands, along with its king and its fighting men. March around the city once with all the armed men. Do this for six days. Have seven priests carry trumpets of rams' horns in front of the ark. On the seventh day, march around the city seven times, with the priests blowing the trumpets. When you hear them sound a long blast on the trumpets, have all the people give a loud shout; then the wall of the city will collapse and the people will go up, every man straight in."'
Joshua 6:1–5

Jericho, probably the world's oldest city, is inseparably linked with Joshua's exploit, undertaken according to the instructions he received from God. The city is exceptional for its deep location; it is situated some 800 feet (230 metres) below sea-level, and about seven miles (eleven kilometres) north of the Dead Sea. In summer it suffers a tropical heat, and in winter is considerably warmer than the surrounding hills. It was the presence of springs of water that helped attract early settlers; today it remains an oasis in a parched region.

Although archaeologists have found evidence for twenty successive settlements at the Tell es Sultan (**aerial photograph**) with the earliest dating from around 8000 BC, Jericho only enters the biblical story with its surveillance and capture by Joshua, following the entry of the Israelites into the Promised Land. It was vitally important to take Jericho, since it represented the key to the control of the surrounding hill country. Joshua first

sent two spies into the city, then proceeded to follow God's instructions, with the predicted result.

Jericho apparently remained desolate until King Ahab rebuilt it in the ninth century BC; the prophets Elijah and Elisha visited the city during his reign. Later Herod the Great built a winter palace in Jericho, since it offered an attractively temperate climate.

We know that Jesus visited the city on his last journey from Galilee to Jerusalem. It was here that he healed blind Bartimaeus, and two other blind men, who greeted him as 'Lord, Son of David' (Mark 10:46–52). Jesus located his story of the Good Samaritan on the winding, arduous road from Jerusalem down to Jericho; and it was in Jericho that he encountered the little tax-collector Zacchaeus, who was so eager to see Jesus that he climbed a sycamore-fig tree.

The Tell has been investigated by a number of archaeologists over the last seventy years. Of particular importance has been the work of the British scholars John Garstang and Dame Kathleen Kenyon, though unfortunately they have been able to throw little light on the Jericho of Joshua's time. Almost nothing seems to remain from that period.

Rising strikingly above Jericho is the Mount of Temptation, traditionally the site of Jesus' tempting by the devil. In the late nineteenth century, the Greek Orthodox church built a spectacular monastery half-way up the mountain (**inset**).

Beth Shan

'The next day, when the Philistines came to strip the dead, they found King Saul and his three sons fallen on Mount Gilboa. They cut off his head and stripped off his armour, and they sent messengers throughout the land of the Philistines to proclaim the news in the temple of their idols and among their people. They put his armour in the temple of the Ashtoreths and fastened his body to the wall of Beth Shan.

'When the people of Jabesh Gilead heard of what the Philistines had done to Saul, all their valiant men journeyed through the night to Beth Shan. They took down the bodies of Saul and his sons from the wall of Beth Shan and went to Jabesh, where they burned them.'
1 Samuel 31:8–12

Beth Shan (or Beth-shean) was situated in the territory of Manasseh, one of the tribes of Israel, but when the Israelites conquered and occupied the Promised Land, they failed to drive out the Canaanites from this town. The place apparently dates back as far as 3500 BC, and eighteen distinct periods of settlement have been identified in the tell, or mound, there by investigating archaeologists (**main photograph**).

At one point, the Philistines advanced inland from their coastal territory and took the town, dedicating a temple to Astarte (Ashtoreth). It was in this temple that they triumphantly hung Saul's armour as a trophy, following his defeat and death in the battle on nearby Mount Gilboa. (This was the battle which occasioned David's famous lament for Jonathan: 'How the mighty have fallen in battle …' 2 Samuel 1:19–27.)

In New Testament times, Beth Shan was occupied by military veterans from the province of Scythia, and became known as Scythopolis. In 63 BC the Roman general Pompey decreed Scythopolis a free city, and it joined the Decapolis league of cities. Under the Romans, Beth Shan flourished, with a thriving textile industry and agriculture. This prosperity is reflected in the fine Roman theatre (**inset**), which is the best preserved in modern Israel.

Originally built to hold some 5000 spectators, the theatre was constructed during the reign of the Emperor Septimius Severus, late in the second century AD. The lower part of the huge semicircular building is actually cut into the hillside, while the upper part is supported on massive masonry foundations. The lower seats and the wall behind the stage remain in remarkably good repair today.

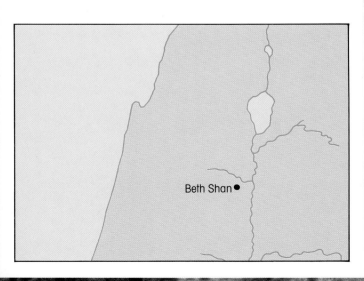

Beth Shan •

Megiddo

'Here is the account of the forced labour King Solomon conscripted to build the LORD's temple, his own palace, the supporting terraces, and Hazor, Megiddo and Gezer.'
1 Kings 9:15

Megiddo was built on the great highway connecting Gaza on the Mediterranean coast with Damascus in the east. It controlled the main pass through the coastal mountains connecting the coastal plains with the valley of Esdraelon. The highway was not only an important trade route, but also of great military significance; in ancient times many armies marched along it from east to west. It is recorded, for instance, that Thutmoses III of Egypt defeated an eastern coalition led by the king of Kadesh at Megiddo; the Egyptian ruler apparently regarded the capture of Megiddo as equal in value to the capture of a thousand towns.

When the Israelites occupied Canaan, Megiddo was in the territory allocated to the tribe of Manasseh; however, the tribe failed to dislodge the Canaanites from this fortified city. It is not clear when exactly the Israelites did take possession of Megiddo, but by the tenth century BC King Solomon had control of it, and was busy rebuilding and fortifying it, to make it into one of his 'chariot cities'. A hundred years later King Ahaziah of Israel, struck by an arrow shot by Jehu, managed to reach the fortress of Megiddo, but died there. King Josiah also died here, after having been wounded in battle. His servants later carried his body from Megiddo to Jerusalem, where he was buried 'in his own sepulchre' (2 Kings 23:30).

The impressive tell at Megiddo (**aerial photograph**) was first excavated in 1905, and as many as twenty distinct settlement levels have been uncovered. The earliest important find was a small Canaanite shrine containing a limestone altar and dating from around 2000 BC. Among other interesting archaeological discoveries has been a great hoard of more than 200 carved ivory objects found in an underground treasury. This form of art was well known in parts of the Middle East in the Iron Age.

From the same period, around 1450 BC, dates the impressive water supply system for the city, consisting of a huge shaft with a staircase around its side, and with a tunnel at its base leading to a spring (**inset**). Archaeologists have also discovered a series of stables extensive enough to accommodate about 450 horses. At first it was assumed that these dated from Solomon's time, and were connected with his chariot forces, but it is now thought more likely that the stables are King Ahab's work. Ahab is known to have had a chariot force consisting of some 2000 vehicles.

'Armageddon', from the Hebrew for Mount Megiddo, is the word used in Revelation for the final battleground between the forces of good and evil. It is fitting that the name of Megiddo, site of so many bloody encounters, should be used in this way.

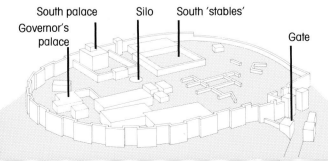

South palace   Silo   South 'stables'
Governor's palace   Gate

Dead Sea

'...Then the boundary will go down along the Jordan and end at the Salt Sea. This will be your land, with its boundaries on every side.'
Numbers 34:12

The Dead Sea is usually referred to in the Bible as the Salt Sea. No water flows out of this inland lake. With the constant high temperatures in this region, there is a rapid rate of evaporation, which means that the lake usually maintains a constant size. The other result of rapid evaporation is that the water is very high in salt content — the Dead Sea has roughly four times the salt concentration of ocean water. As is well known, this high salinity means that the water is extraordinarily buoyant; tourists enjoy 'sitting' on its surface.

The other remarkable feature of the Dead Sea is its low altitude. The surface of the water is lower than that of any other area of water on the earth, and lies 1290 feet (390 metres) below sea-level. The Dead Sea is situated in the floor of the Jordan Rift Valley, with steep cliffs rising some 1500–2500 feet (450–750 metres) to the east and west. The Dead Sea is about 47 miles (76 kilometres) long, and up to ten miles (sixteen kilometres) wide. Towards its southern end there is a small peninsula jutting out; the area south of this was probably not part of the lake in biblical times, and the 'cities of the plain' referred to in the book of Genesis may have been located here.

Five 'cities of the plain' are mentioned in Genesis: Sodom, Gomorrah, Admah, Zeboiim and Zoar. When Lot and Abraham decided to divide the land between them, Abraham let Lot have first choice. The younger man saw that the valley was the more fertile area, and settled there with his family. Today the region could hardly be described as 'fertile', but the traces of many water courses have been found which would have made the plain much more fertile in ancient times.

It was, then, somewhere south of the Dead Sea that the famous incident occurred when Lot escaped from the destruction of Sodom and Gomorrah. Only Lot and his wife and daughters escaped, and, as is well-known, his wife looked back to the home they had left and was turned to salt. A salt cave near the presumed site of Sodom is said to be Lot's wife. The story in Genesis 19 came to symbolize God's judgment on the wicked; Jesus referred to Sodom when he condemned the town of Capernaum for its unbelief in his own day (Matthew 11:23–24).

In the main photograph the barren Judean foothills can be seen in the foreground; beyond the Dead Sea, to the east, are the hills of Moab, in modern Jordan. In biblical times the region of TransJordan was the home of small nations such as the Moabites, the Edomites, the Ammonites and Syrians. According to Genesis 19, Moab and Ammon were founded by the daughters of Lot.

Inset: The Judean foothills near the Dead Sea; three ibex stand on the skyline.

Dead Sea

Qumran

In the summer of 1947, a young bedouin goatherd who had lost one of his flock was searching in the cliffs overlooking the Dead Sea, when he stumbled upon a cave full of scrolls. He came from the Ta'amin tribe, and, once they realized he might have discovered something of importance, the tribesmen took some of their finds to Bethlehem. Five scrolls eventually reached the United States, where they were sold to an anonymous buyer for $250,000. The buyer was none other than the Israeli general and leading archaeologist, the late Yigael Yadin. Later five additional scrolls were purchased for Israel in Jerusalem, while Jordan acquired two copper scrolls from the same source.

In total more than 500 manuscripts have been discovered in the caves at Qumran — some in Aramaic, some in Hebrew and a few in Greek. Most are on parchment rolls, which were stored in clay pots to help preserve them. The dry air of the Dead Sea region has also helped prevent the deterioration of the scrolls.

The prime importance of the Dead Sea Scrolls is that they represent the oldest copies we have of the Bible. They include all the books of the Old Testament, except Esther, and have been invaluable to scholars in showing the reliability of the text of the Bible. The great American archaeologist W.F. Albright reckoned that Qumran yielded the 'greatest find of manuscripts in modern times'. The texts also included records of the Essene sect, a Jewish group which objected to much of the Temple worship in Jerusalem, and which set up a community at Qumran. Their monastery at Qumran, which has been thoroughly excavated, was set up around 150 BC and was finally destroyed by the Romans in AD 68, during the Jewish War.

The Essenes living at Qumran were strict and ascetic in their lifestyle. New members were required to give all their possessions to the community, and were received into the sect by baptism. They devoted their time to praising God in hymns and psalms, and to reading their Scriptures. They even had a ceremonial meal, in which bread was broken and wine offered up.

The monastery at Qumran comprises a cluster of buildings, including a tower near the entrance, an assembly hall, and a special room set aside for the copying of manuscripts by scribes. There were a number of cisterns and pools, both for the provision of drinking water and for the baptism ceremony. Near the monastery are spectacular cliffs (**inset**) honeycombed with caves, in eleven of which the amazing discovery of the scrolls was made.

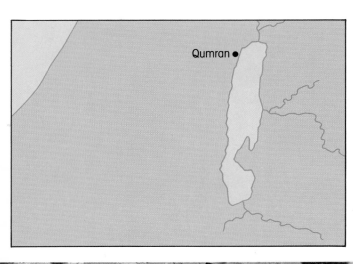

Nazareth

'In the sixth month, God sent the angel Gabriel to Nazareth, a town in Galilee, to a virgin pledged to a man named Joseph, a descendant of David. The virgin's name was Mary. The angel went to her and said, "Greetings, you who are highly favoured! The Lord is with you."

'Mary was greatly troubled at his words and wondered what kind of greeting this might be. But the angel said to her, "Do not be afraid, Mary, you have found favour with God. You will be with child and give birth to a son, and you are to give him the name Jesus. He will be great and will be called the Son of the Most High. The Lord God will give him the throne of his father David, and he will reign over the house of Jacob for ever; his kingdom will never end."' Luke 1:26–33

Despite its later fame, Nazareth is not mentioned in the Old Testament; it was probably only a small village of little significance. Even at the time of Christ, people tended to look down on it; Nathaniel asked, 'Nazareth! Can anything good come from there?' (John 1:46).

Yet it was in this town, nestling in the hills of lower Galilee, that Mary was living when she received the momentous message from the angel. After the birth of Jesus in Bethlehem, Joseph and Mary fled to Egypt to escape the persecution of Herod the Great. The Holy Family then considered returning to Bethlehem, but were deterred when they heard that Herod's son, Archelaus, had succeeded to the throne. They decided to make the journey back to Nazareth instead.

So it was in this town that Jesus grew up. Following his baptism by John the Baptist, he read the scriptures at the Nazareth synagogue, but his message only succeeded in angering the congregation, who attempted to throw him off a nearby cliff.

The modern Franciscan Church of the Annunciation (**aerial photograph**) stands over the site of the Grotto of the Annunciation, which has been honoured as the site of Mary's visitation by the angel from as early as the third century AD, when a simple church was built there. Soon after this the Empress Helena, mother of the Christian emperor Constantine, built a second church on the same spot.

Although Helena's church was destroyed by the Persians in 614, in the twelfth century Tancred, prince of Galilee, built a considerably grander church, which in its turn was destroyed by invaders. The fourth church on the site was not started until the eighteenth century, when the Franciscans built their first sanctuary here, only to demolish it in 1955 to make way for the present magnificent structure, designed by the Italian architect Giovanni Muzio. The modern building is largely constructed over the foundations of Tancred's crusader church, and has a large opening in the floor through which visitors can look down to the grotto beneath. The church has been richly decorated with mosaics, doors and windows created by artists from many different parts of the world.

Inset: Detail of 'The Annunciation' by Max Ingrand, from the west window of the Church of the Annunciation.

Bethlehem

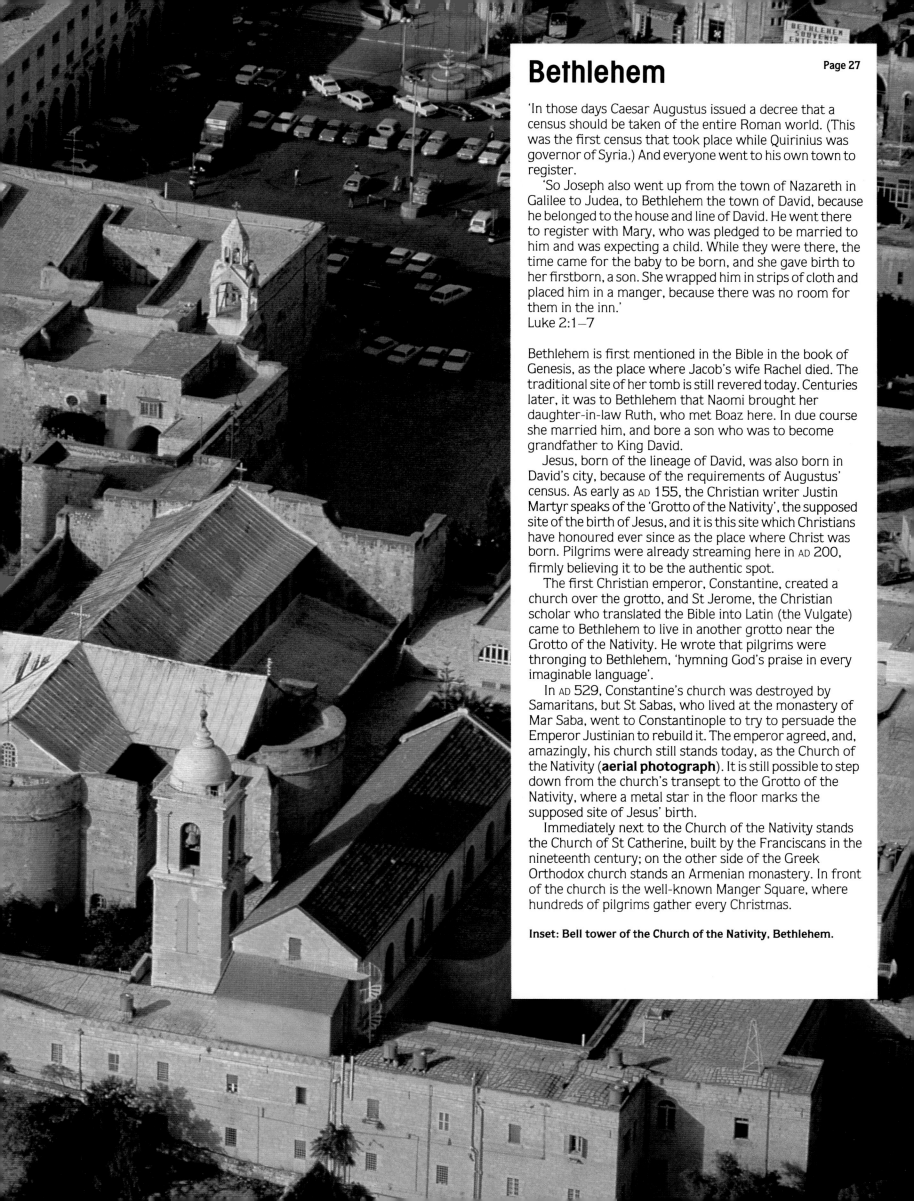

Bethlehem

'In those days Caesar Augustus issued a decree that a census should be taken of the entire Roman world. (This was the first census that took place while Quirinius was governor of Syria.) And everyone went to his own town to register.

'So Joseph also went up from the town of Nazareth in Galilee to Judea, to Bethlehem the town of David, because he belonged to the house and line of David. He went there to register with Mary, who was pledged to be married to him and was expecting a child. While they were there, the time came for the baby to be born, and she gave birth to her firstborn, a son. She wrapped him in strips of cloth and placed him in a manger, because there was no room for them in the inn.'
Luke 2:1–7

Bethlehem is first mentioned in the Bible in the book of Genesis, as the place where Jacob's wife Rachel died. The traditional site of her tomb is still revered today. Centuries later, it was to Bethlehem that Naomi brought her daughter-in-law Ruth, who met Boaz here. In due course she married him, and bore a son who was to become grandfather to King David.

Jesus, born of the lineage of David, was also born in David's city, because of the requirements of Augustus' census. As early as AD 155, the Christian writer Justin Martyr speaks of the 'Grotto of the Nativity', the supposed site of the birth of Jesus, and it is this site which Christians have honoured ever since as the place where Christ was born. Pilgrims were already streaming here in AD 200, firmly believing it to be the authentic spot.

The first Christian emperor, Constantine, created a church over the grotto, and St Jerome, the Christian scholar who translated the Bible into Latin (the Vulgate) came to Bethlehem to live in another grotto near the Grotto of the Nativity. He wrote that pilgrims were thronging to Bethlehem, 'hymning God's praise in every imaginable language'.

In AD 529, Constantine's church was destroyed by Samaritans, but St Sabas, who lived at the monastery of Mar Saba, went to Constantinople to try to persuade the Emperor Justinian to rebuild it. The emperor agreed, and, amazingly, his church still stands today, as the Church of the Nativity (**aerial photograph**). It is still possible to step down from the church's transept to the Grotto of the Nativity, where a metal star in the floor marks the supposed site of Jesus' birth.

Immediately next to the Church of the Nativity stands the Church of St Catherine, built by the Franciscans in the nineteenth century; on the other side of the Greek Orthodox church stands an Armenian monastery. In front of the church is the well-known Manger Square, where hundreds of pilgrims gather every Christmas.

Inset: Bell tower of the Church of the Nativity, Bethlehem.

River Jordan

'Then Jesus came from Galilee to the Jordan to be baptised by John. But John tried to deter him, saying, "I need to be baptised by you, and do you come to me?"

'Jesus replied, "Let it be so now; it is proper for us to do this to fulfil all righteousness." Then John consented.

'As soon as Jesus was baptised, he went up out of the water. At that moment heaven was opened, and he saw the spirit of God descending like a dove and lighting on him. And a voice from heaven said, "This is my Son, whom I love; with him I am well pleased."'
Matthew 3:13—17

The river Jordan is the only major river in Israel, and has always taken an important part in the history of the land, as well as a significant symbolic role.

In the Old Testament by far the most important event relating to the River Jordan was the crossing made by the Israelites after the death of Moses. This crossing symbolized their taking possession of the Promised Land: 'The LORD your God has given you this land to take possession of it. But all your able-bodied men, armed for battle, must cross over ahead of your brother Israelites ...' (Deuteronomy 3:18).

The story of the crossing is told in the book of Joshua:

'So when the people broke camp to cross the Jordan, the priests carrying the ark of the covenant went ahead of them. Now the Jordan is in flood all during harvest. Yet as soon as the priests who carried the ark reached the Jordan and their feet touched the water's edge, the water from upstream stopped flowing. It piled up in a heap a great distance away ... So the people crossed over opposite Jericho. The priests who carried the ark of the covenant of the LORD stood firm on dry ground in the middle of Jordan, while all Israel passed by until the whole nation had completed the crossing on dry ground.'
Joshua 3:14—17

In the New Testament, the only direct reference to the Jordan is related to John the Baptist's ministry, and his baptism of Jesus.

The distance, as the crow flies, from the point where the Jordan leaves the Sea of Galilee to the point where it joins the Dead Sea is only 70 miles (110 kilometres); yet, so much does it twist and meander, that the river is in fact 200 miles (320 kilometres) long. It is not a particularly deep river — it varies from three to ten feet (one to three metres) in depth and is up to 90 feet (thirty metres) wide. Between the Sea of Galilee and the Dead Sea there are as many as twenty-seven rapids; for this reason the river has never been navigable.

Inset: The river Jordan at sunrise.

Limestone relief of the star of David, from the third-century synagogue at Capernaum.

Capernaum

'When Jesus heard that John had been put in prison, he returned to Galilee. Leaving Nazareth, he went and lived in Capernaum, which was by the lake in the area of Zebulun and Naphtali — to fulfil what was said through the prophet Isaiah:
'"Land of Zebulun and land of Naphtali,
the way to the sea, along the Jordan,
Galilee of the Gentiles —
the people living in darkness have seen a great light;
on those living in the land of the shadow of death
a light has dawned."'
'From that time on Jesus began to preach, "Repent, for the kingdom of heaven is near."'
Matthew 4:12–17

Although Jesus was brought up in Nazareth, he made the lakeside town of Capernaum his headquarters during his ministry in Galilee. Capernaum was the home of the tax-collector Levi — also known as Matthew — and of the Roman officer whose paralyzed servant Jesus healed.

It was in Capernaum, too, that Jesus performed a number of other healing miracles, including the healing of the paralytic who was lowered to Jesus through an opening in the roof; the royal official's son; Peter's mother-in-law, who was confined to bed with a fever; and many others who were sick.

In recent years archaeologists have excavated extensively on the site of the biblical town of Capernaum, and have discovered much of interest. In Jesus' time, Capernaum was the largest of some thirty fishing towns situated around the lake, and was near the important main road heading south to Egypt and east into Syria. Jesus chose a busy centre for his ministry.

However, apart from the ruins, no city now exists on the site. Jesus prophesied: 'And you, Capernaum, will you be lifted up to the skies? No, you will go down to the depths' (Matthew 11:23–24).

One of the most important finds in Capernaum has been a white limestone synagogue, which has been partially reconstructed from the scattered remains (**aerial photograph**). It is a major attraction for modern tourists, since we know that Jesus preached in the Capernaum synagogue (Mark 1:21–22). However, this building dates from at least as late as the third century AD, and cannot possibly be the building that Jesus knew. Recently Franciscan archaeologists have discovered the remains of an earlier building, made of local black basalt, beneath the limestone synagogue. This building, which seems to date from the first century AD, has a cobbled stone floor and elegant cornices, and may well be the actual synagogue where Jesus once preached, and which was built by a Roman centurion living here (Luke 7:1–5).

Artist's reconstruction of the third-century synagogue, Capernaum.

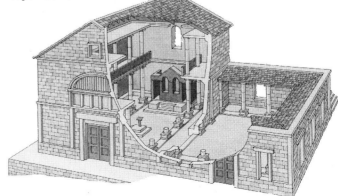

Sea of Galilee

'One day Jesus said to his disciples, "Let's go over to the other side of the lake." So they got into a boat and set out. As they sailed, he fell asleep. A squall came down on the lake, so that the boat was being swamped, and they were in great danger.

'The disciples went and woke him, saying, "Master, Master, we're going to drown!"

'He got up and rebuked the wind and the raging waters; the storm subsided, and all was calm. "Where is your faith?" he asked his disciples.

'In fear and amazement they asked one another, "Who is this? He commands even the winds and the water, and they obey him."'
Luke 8:22–25

The Sea of Galilee has been known by a number of different names, all of them derived from places on its west shore (Galilee is the region west of the lake). It has been known as the Sea of Gennesaret, from the Plain of Gennesaret to the north-west; the Sea of Chinnereth, from the town of this name on its shore (or from its harp shape – Chinnereth is the Hebrew for 'harp-shaped'); and the Sea of Tiberias, from Herod Antipas' capital on the west shore.

A number of writers have noticed that the lake can experience sudden and violent storms. These result from cold air sweeping down from the plateau of Gaulanitis (the Golan Heights) and from Hermon and converging at the head of the lake, where it meets warm air.

Today's visitor to Galilee is impressed by the lake's serenity and calm; there are few settlements of any size around it, apart from the thriving resort of Tiberias. Christians tend to ponder on the tranquillity and the silence. However, the picture has changed drastically since Jesus' time. In his day there was a string of busy towns around the lake, and the sea would have been crowded with fishing vessels and other commercial craft. Jesus seems to have centred his ministry around three particular lake towns: Capernaum, Chorazim and Bethsaida-Philippi.

It is fascinating that in 1961 an archaeological expedition turned up an old shoreline some fifteen feet (five metres) below the water, near the site of Magdala. Further searching in the mud revealed twenty-nine cooking pots, together with an assortment of dishes, juglets and two stone anchors. Although no other remains have survived, it seems that the earthenware represents the cargo of a boat that foundered on the lake in the first century – possibly as a result of one of the sudden squalls.

Although Tiberias was an important and magnificent city at that time, we have no record that Jesus ever entered it. Some scholars have suggested this was because orthodox Jews of his day considered it unclean; but it is more likely that he was avoiding the unwelcome attentions of Herod Antipas.

Inset: Fishing at sunrise on the Sea of Galilee.

Mount of Beatitudes

'Now when he saw the crowds, he went up on a mountainside and sat down. His disciples came to him, and he began to teach them, saying:
'"Blessed are the poor in spirit, for theirs is the kingdom of heaven.
Blessed are those who mourn, for they will be comforted.
Blessed are the meek, for they will inherit the earth.
Blessed are those who hunger and thirst for righteousness, for they will be filled.
Blessed are the merciful, for they will be shown mercy.
Blessed are the pure in heart, for they will see God.
Blessed are the peacemakers, for they will be called sons of God.
Blessed are those who are persecuted because of righteousness, for theirs is the kingdom of heaven.
Blessed are you when people insult you, persecute you and falsely say all kinds of evil against you because of me. Rejoice and be glad, because great is your reward in heaven, for in the same way they persecuted the prophets who were before you."'
Matthew 5:1–12

The Mount of Beatitudes is by tradition the place where Jesus delivered the Sermon on the Mount. The hill is on the north shore of the Sea of Galilee, just above the site of Capernaum, and commands a magnificent view across the lake. Whether or not it is the true site of the Sermon on the Mount, it allows the modern visitor to imagine the original scene.

In earlier years a church stood some way down the hill, but in 1937 this was replaced by the present building, with its pleasant arches and shady gardens. Each of the church's eight sides is inscribed in Latin with one of the eight beatitudes of Matthew 5, while the dome itself is held to symbolize the ninth and crowning beatitude.

Not far from the Mount of Beatitudes, by the lakeside, stands the Church of the Multiplication of the Loaves and Fishes, commemorating the feeding of the four thousand (Matthew 15:29–39). As early as AD 382 a pilgrim named Pelagia found a church standing on this site. Today's church is built over the remains of a Byzantine building, and inside it the visitor can see well-preserved remains of that church's mosaic flooring. As well as the general intricate depiction of the birds and flowers of Lake Galilee — herons, doves, geese, ducks, peacocks, lotuses, oleanders and the rest — there is a basket with five loaves and two fish (**inset**) — an early commemoration of the feeding of the four thousand (Mark 8:1–8).

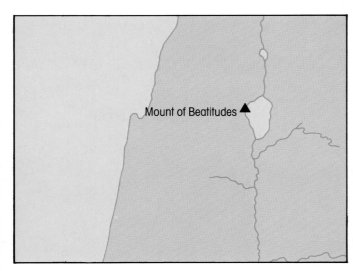

Mount of Beatitudes ▲

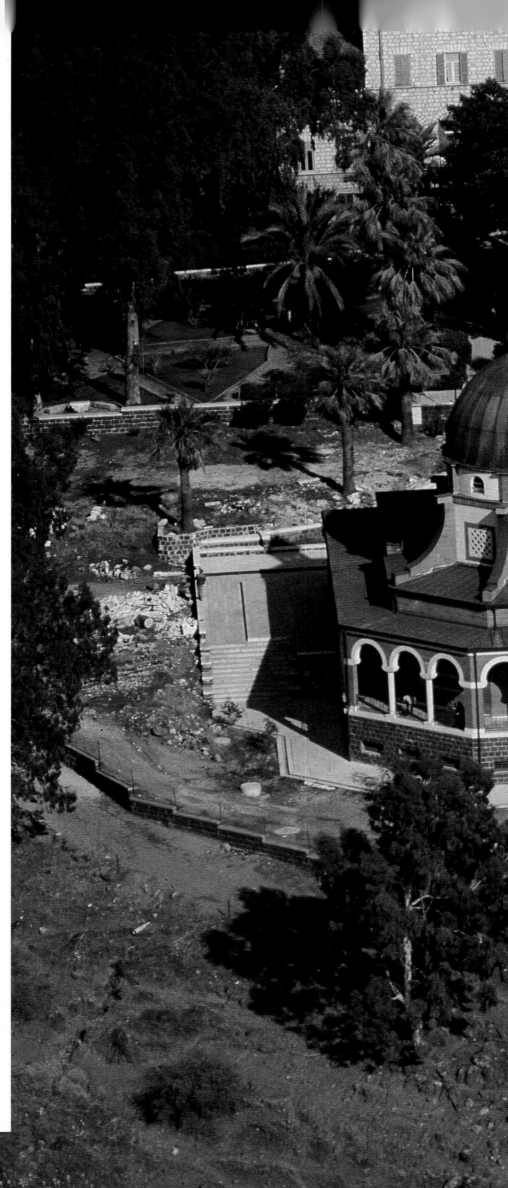

Galilee

Only one of the lakeside towns of Jesus' day survives as a modern settlement – Tiberias. On the western shores of the lake, the Israelis have been able to cultivate the land intensively to produce such crops as bananas, oranges and grapes (**aerial photograph**).

In New Testament times a number of cities were situated on the east side of the lake. These included two cities belonging to the Decapolis confederation, Hippos and Gadara. Hippos was built on the hilltop, directly across the lake from the city of Tiberias, which in Roman times it rivalled for importance. Today impressive remains may still be seen, including streets, public buildings, mosaic floors and massive red columns.

South-west of Hippos are the remains of the second Decapolis city, Gadara, and its warm-spring resort, Hammat Gadara. The amazing bath complex at Hammat Gadara probably dates from around the beginning of the third century AD, and remained in use for centuries.

One of the most-disputed locations in the Gospel story is that for the incident when Jesus cast demons into a herd of swine (Matthew 8:28, Mark 5:1–20, Luke 8:26–39). In some New Testament manuscripts, the incident is said to have taken place in 'the country of the Gadarenes', indicating the lakeside territories of the city of Gadara; other manuscripts speak of 'the country of the Gerasenes', pointing to Gerasa, thirty miles away.

However, yet other manuscripts talk of 'the country of the Gergesenes', indicating a completely different site. The Byzantine church apparently believed this to be some miles north of Hippos, at el-Kursi, where the hills drop particularly steeply towards the lake. To commemorate the incident, they built a large monastery and church here (**inset**). The church has been carefully excavated in recent times, and archaeologists also discovered a tower enclosing a large boulder built on the hillside. The excavators believe that for the Byzantine Christians the boulder probably had some significance in marking the miracle.

The Sea of Galilee looking north-west towards Magdala.

Capernaum

Magdala

Tiberias

Chorazin

Gadara

Bethsaida

Sea of Galilee

Caesarea Philippi

'Jesus and his disciples went on to the villages around Caesarea Philippi. On the way he asked them, "Who do people say I am?"

'They replied, "Some say John the Baptist; others say Elijah; and still others, one of the prophets." "But what about you?" he asked. "Who do you say I am?"

'Peter answered, "You are the Christ."

'Jesus warned them not to tell anyone about him.'
Mark 8:27–30

Caesarea Philippi was situated at the northernmost boundary of Palestine, just as its modern counterpart Baniyas is at the northern frontier of modern Israel, among the foothills of Mount Hermon, a beautiful wooded area some thirty miles (forty-eight kilometres) from the Mediterranean coast.

There has been a settlement on this site from early times; possibly it is to be identified with the Baal-gad mentioned in the book of Joshua. For centuries the place became a centre for the worship of the god Pan, who seems to have replaced Baal as the local deity. The cult of Pan, Greek god of fertility, was linked with the spring where the Jordan rises, near an impressive high rock wall (**aerial photograph**). It was from the name Pan that the place gained its ancient name 'Paneas' — and the modern name Baniyas. There are a number of niches and openings carved into the cliff-face, where images were presumably once located (**inset**). Some of the niches still have their original inscriptions in Greek.

Baniyas has its importance in political history; it was here in 200 BC that Antiochus III defeated the Ptolemaean forces, thereby adding Palestine to the Seleucid empire. The Roman Emperor Augustus presented the region to Herod the Great, whose son Philip built his capital here. Philip named the place Caesarea Philippi, to distinguish it from Caesarea Maritima, on the coast.

It was near here that Peter made his confession of Jesus as the Christ; it is particularly fitting that his unequivocal statement came in a place dedicated to the pagan deity, Pan. Matthew's account tells of Jesus' response to Peter's confession of Jesus as the 'Son of the living God': '"Blessed are you, Simon son of Jonah, for this was not revealed to you by man, but by my Father in heaven. And I tell you that you are Peter, and on this rock I will build my church, and the gates of Hades will not overcome it "' (Matthew 16:17–18).

It was shortly after this that Jesus took Peter, James and John up a high mountain, where they witnessed his transfiguration. Some commentators have claimed that this took place on nearby Mount Hermon, although another tradition locates the transfiguration on Mount Tabor.

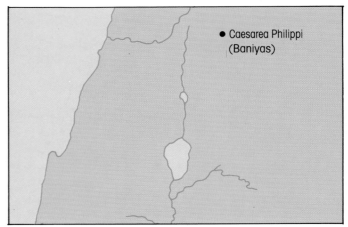

● Caesarea Philippi
(Baniyas)

Mount Tabor

'After six days Jesus took Peter, James and John with him
and led them up a high mountain, where they were all
alone. There he was transfigured before them. His clothes
became dazzling white, whiter than anyone in the world
could bleach them. And there appeared before them Elijah
and Moses, who were talking with Jesus.

'Peter said to Jesus, "Rabbi, it is good for us to be here.
Let us put up three shelters — one for you, one for Moses
and one for Elijah." (He did not know what to say, they
were so frightened.)

'Then a cloud appeared and enveloped them, and a voice
came from the cloud: "This is my Son, whom I love. Listen
to him!"

'Suddenly, when they looked round, they no longer saw
anyone with them except Jesus.'
Mark 9:2—8

Mount Tabor is by tradition the site of the transfiguration
of Jesus. As early as 2000 BC the Canaanites set up a shrine
or 'high place' for the worship of Baal on the summit of
Tabor. The hill has an unmistakable profile, and rises some
1938 feet (588 metres) to command a magnificent view
over the vale of Jezreel, west towards Nazareth, south
towards Samaria, east to the Jordan rift valley, and north
towards Galilee.

During the time when the Judges were ruling Israel, it
was on Mount Tabor that Deborah and Barak, the
prophetess and the general, mustered their army before
advancing to overrun the enemy: 'So Barak went down
Mount Tabor, followed by ten thousand men. At Barak's
advance, the LORD routed Sisera and all his chariots and
army by the sword, and Sisera abandoned his chariot and
fled on foot' (Judges 4:14—15).

It is from the fourth century AD that Christians began to
link Mount Tabor with the Gospel accounts of the
transfiguration, and by 422 there were churches on the
mountain. When the Crusaders came to attempt to win
back the Holy Places from the Muslims, they built a
fortress on the mountain. In time the Islamic forces
destroyed the Crusader castle, but the Franciscans later
took possession of the site on the summit.

Today two churches stand on top of Mount Tabor: the
Greek Orthodox church of Elijah, built in 1911; and the
Franciscan church, a massively impressive building
designed by the Italian architect Barluzzi, and constructed
in light-coloured limestone (**inset**). The Franciscan church
takes in three chapels which are reputed to be the three
booths that Peter wanted to erect after the
transfiguration.

Mount Tabor ▲

Samaria

'Now Jesus had to go through Samaria. So he came to a town in Samaria called Sychar, near the plot of ground Jacob had given to his son Joseph. Jacob's well was there, and Jesus, tired as he was from the journey, sat down by the well. It was about the sixth hour.

'When a Samaritan woman came to draw water, Jesus said to her, "Will you give me a drink?" (His disciples had gone into the town to buy food.)

'The Samaritan woman said to him, "You are a Jew and I am a Samaritan woman. How can you ask me for a drink?" ...

'Jesus answered her, "If you knew the gift of God, and who it is that asks you for a drink, you would have asked him and he would have given you living water."'
John 4:4–10

Lying north of the Dead Sea and west of the river Jordan is the hill country of Samaria — known today as the West Bank. This is a rugged, mountainous region, crossed by valleys and ravines, stretching from the Jordan valley to the Plain of Sharon in the west to the valley of Jezreel and Esdraelon in the north, and merging into the Judean hills in the south. A number of mountain passes give access through Samaria, including the important routes from Beth Shan to Megiddo.

Samaria features in the biblical narrative from earliest times. Both Abraham and his grandson Jacob built altars at Shechem in Samaria. Later, when Joshua led the conquest of the Promised Land, the Israelites buried the bones of Joseph, which they had carried with them all the way from Egypt, in the land which Jacob had bought at Shechem years before.

It was in Samaria, too, that several of the judges of Israel were active, including the prophetess Deborah, Gideon, who delivered his people from the Midianites, Tola and Abdon. The prophet Samuel grew up at the tabernacle at Shiloh, which is probably to be identified with the Arab village of Seilun, south of Shechem. Later Samuel moved to his birthplace Ramah, and travelled to a number of towns in the region, such as Bethel, Gilgal and Mizpah.

When the kingdom divided, Israel, the northern kingdom, made the town of Samaria its capital. It offered a strategic view over the surrounding area, and Omri strengthened it into a formidable fortress which took the Assyrians three years to reduce (723–721 BC).

The notorious King Ahab and Queen Jezebel also made Samaria their capital, where their extravagant ways and pagan practices provoked the condemnation of the prophets Amos, Micah, Isaiah and Hosea. When the Assyrians duly invaded, the entire population was deported, and alien Assyrians were introduced to garrison the stronghold.

Later, Herod built the town of Sebaste over part of the site of Samaria, using a Graeco-Roman style of architecture.

Sychar, the place of Jesus' meeting with the Samaritan woman, has often been identified with modern Sichem (Shechem), although it is not possible to know for certain where it was.

Inset: A woman olive-picker in Samaria.

Mount Gerizim

Mount Gerizim, which rises to a height of 2849 feet (860 metres), has played an important role in the story of Israel, and particularly in the story of the Samaritans. It towers above a major routeway running north-south from Jerusalem to Galilee, and has always had a strategic significance.

Moses laid down that, when the Israelites came to enter the Promised Land, the blessing for keeping the law should be pronounced from the summit of Mount Gerizim; similarly, the curse for disobeying the law was to be pronounced from the peak of the neighbouring Mount Ebal. Six of the tribes of Israel were to stand on each mountain. It was from the peak of Mount Gerizim, too, that Jotham shouted his parable about the trees to the citizens of Shechem (modern Nablus) below, condemning them for making Abimelech king, and for forgetting the achievements of his father, Gideon, in driving the Midianites from the land.

When the Israelites returned from exile in Babylon, they found that Samaria had become inhabited by people of mixed race, and refused to allow them to participate in the reconstruction of Jerusalem and the rebuilding of the temple. Excluded in this way, the Samaritans set about building a temple of their own on Mount Gerizim. Although this building was later destroyed by the Maccabees, the Samaritans continued to worship in the open air on the summit of Mount Gerizim. In Jesus' meeting with the Samaritan woman at the well at Sychar, she refers to Mount Gerizim: 'Our fathers worshipped on this mountain, but you Jews claim that the place where we must worship is in Jerusalem' (John 4:20).

Even today the small Samaritan community living in Nablus, sited under the shadow of the mountain, climb Mount Gerizim each year to celebrate the passover. The Samaritans even claim that it was on this mountain that Abraham attempted to sacrifice his son, Isaac, and that it was here that Jacob dreamed of the ladder leading to heaven.

Today on the summit stand ruins of a stronghold built by the Emperor Justinian in AD 633 (**aerial photograph**), as well as a stone which the Samaritans claim is the altar from their temple.

Shechem (modern Nablus) is the first place in the Bible to be mentioned in connection with Abraham's arrival in the Promised Land, and it recurs frequently throughout the book of Genesis. It was at Shechem, too, that Joseph's brothers were herding the flocks of their father Jacob, when Joseph was sent to check on their well-being. Later, it was to Shechem that Solomon's son, Rehoboam, came to be made king by all Israel, whilst Jeroboam made it his capital when he led the breakaway of the ten tribes from Rehoboam.

Inset: A stone watch-tower in Samaria.

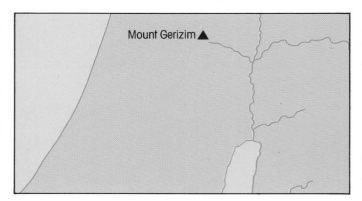

Jerusalem

Jerusalem is a city unique in its importance to three great world religions – Judaism, Islam and Christianity. It is the city of David and Solomon, and the site of their temple; it is the city where Jesus was tried, crucified, and rose again; it is the city revered by Muslims as the place from which Muhammad ascended into heaven. The old city of Jerusalem still has the atmosphere and appearance of a Middle Eastern town of the past, with its narrow crowded streets, noisy bazaar and jostling population.

Archaeologists have found traces of life on this site from as early as the Old Stone Age, and by 3000 BC people had settled on Mount Ophel, south of the present Temple Mount area. The Canaanites established a town here, known as Salem at the time when Abraham visited it and was welcomed by its priest-king Melchizedek.

When King David captured the city it had been in the hands of the Jebusites. Under his rule Jerusalem, built around Mount Ophel, became the religious and political centre of the kingdom, although it was not until the reign of his son Solomon that the temple was built, along with a new royal palace. When the kingdom divided, after the

death of Solomon, Jerusalem remained the capital of the southern kingdom.

King Hezekiah, a great reformer, cleansed the temple after it had been defiled by the worship of Assyrian gods, constructed defensive walls around the city, and built a special tunnel to ensure a water supply even during time of siege. In 587 BC came the catastrophe of the capture of the city by the Babylonians, and the captivity of Judah. The city was laid waste and the temple destroyed. It was not till after the return from captivity that the walls were rebuilt and the Second Temple constructed, under the leadership of Nehemiah. There followed a period of Greek domination, followed by the Roman occupation.

When Herod the Great came to power in 37 BC, he set about a major programme of public building, including a great royal palace for himself, and the magnificent reconstruction of the temple, all in a Graeco-Roman style. It was Herod's city that Jesus knew – a city of palaces, amphitheatres, baths, markets and above all the great temple. Agrippa I enlarged the city still further, but Jerusalem was razed to the ground in AD 70 by the

Roman general Titus during the Jewish War. The temple was assaulted and almost totally demolished.

Later the Emperor Hadrian rebuilt the city, naming it Aelia Capitolina. Under Constantine, the first Christian emperor, several churches were built, some on the believed sites of important events in the Gospel story. Justinian similarly encouraged the building of churches in Jerusalem.

The pattern of conquest continued. Islamic forces took Jerusalem in 638, building the Dome of the Rock and the El Aqsa Mosque; Crusaders held the city for a time; Jews re-entered in the thirteenth century; the British came in 1917; and in 1949 Israel occupied part of the city, taking the remainder in 1967.

Inset: An elderly man at the Western Wall, Jerusalem.

Dome of the Rock

This magnificent building has for many people come to symbolize the city of Jerusalem. It stands over one of the world's most revered sites, of enormous significance for Jews, Christians and Muslims alike. Its history begins with Abraham. When God instructed him to sacrifice his son Isaac, it is generally believed that Mount Moriah, the place of sacrifice, was the place where the Dome of the Rock now stands: 'Some time later God tested Abraham. He said to him, "Abraham!" "Here I am," he replied. Then God said, "Take your son, your only son Isaac, whom you love, and go to the region of Moriah. Sacrifice him there as a burnt offering on one of the mountains"' (Genesis 22:1–2). In fact, the Dome of the Rock covers a 'holy rock' which is held to be the spot where Abraham intended to sacrifice Isaac, until God provided a ram in his place.

When King David captured Jerusalem, he built an altar on the site, and placed the Ark of the Covenant there. It was his son Solomon, however, who built the first temple here, the most magnificent structure in his kingdom, with the altar of burnt offering on top of the Moriah rock.

Four hundred years later, the Babylonians destroyed the temple, when they captured Jerusalem in 587 BC. The Israelites were taken into captivity, and did not return for over fifty years, when they set about building the Second Temple – a considerably less lavish structure.

It was King Herod who proceeded to restore and rebuild the Second Temple in as splendid a manner as he could. He also extended the temple area to its present limits – 985 by 1575 feet (300 by 480 metres). A wonder of its age, this building, too, lasted only a short time, and was destroyed by the Romans during the final rising of the Jews in AD 70.

When the Muslims took the city in 638, Omar, second successor of Muhammad, immediately went to pray on Abraham's Rock. The sumptuous Dome of the Rock, probably built by Abd el Malik (685–701), remains a focal point of the city, with its colourful tiling and gilded roof.

The interior of the Dome of the Rock.

Gethsemane

'They went to a place called Gethsemane, and Jesus said to his disciples, "Sit here while I pray." He took Peter, James and John along with him, and he began to be deeply distressed and troubled.
'"My soul is overwhelmed with sorrow to the point of death," he said to them. "Stay here and keep watch."
'Going a little farther, he fell to the ground and prayed that if possible the hour might pass from him.
'"*Abba*, Father," he said, "everything is possible for you. Take this cup from me. Yet not what I will, but what you will."'
Mark 14:32–36

The name 'Gethsemane' probably comes from the Hebrew for 'oil press', a likely derivation, since the area is thick with olive trees. It was here that Jesus brought his disciples after the Last Supper, and, though he told them to watch and pray, they fell asleep. Eventually a band of armed men, led by Judas, came to find him to take him before the chief priests.

Like so many of the traditional sites of the Holy Land, Gethsemane has been supposed since early times to be located here. In the fourth century, the Emperor Theodosius I built a basilica church over the rock where it was claimed Jesus prayed in the garden. The modern Church of All Nations (**aerial photograph**) is built on the same site, and inside it the original church's floor-plan is still visible. The church derives its name from the fact that pictures in it have been given by Christians from many different lands.

The Church of All Nations is not the only church in this vicinity. Very close to it stands the unmistakably Russian Church of Mary Magdalene (**foreground, aerial photograph**), with its seven onion-shaped domes. The church was built by the Tsar Alexander III in memory of his mother.

A little further away stands the Dominus Flevit Chapel, owned by the Franciscans. Built as recently as 1955, the church stands on the ruins of a fifth-century church. The name of the church is the Latin form of 'The Lord wept', and commemorates Jesus' lament over the city of Jerusalem when he came to the city for the last time:
'As he approached Jerusalem and saw the city, he wept over it and said, "If you, even you, had only known on this day what would bring you peace – but now it is hidden from your eyes"' (Luke 19:41-42).

Within the Garden of Gethsemane today stand eight ancient olive trees, which many people like to believe were growing there in Jesus' day. However, the Jewish historian Josephus claims that the Roman general Titus tore up all the trees surrounding the city of Jerusalem during his desperate siege of the city in the Jewish War of AD 70. In any event, the eight trees are certainly venerable, and help create an appropriate atmosphere.

Inset: An ancient olive tree and cyclamen in the Garden of Gethsemane, Jerusalem.

Citadel

'When Pilate heard this, he brought Jesus out and sat down on the judge's seat at a place known as The Stone Pavement (which in Aramaic is Gabbatha). It was the day of Preparation of Passover Week, about the sixth hour.
'"Here is your king," Pilate said to the Jews. But they shouted, "Take him away! Take him away! Crucify him!"
'"Shall I crucify your king?" Pilate asked.
'"We have no king but Caesar," the chief priests answered.
'Finally Pilate handed Jesus over to them to be crucified.'
John 19:13–16

Alongside the Jaffa Gate into the old city of Jerusalem stands the Citadel, a Turkish fortress. It was on this site that Herod the Great built three huge towers in the years immediately before the birth of Christ, giving each tower a name. They were called Phasael, Hippicus and Mariamne.

When the Roman general Titus finally overcame Jewish resistance in Jerusalem during the Jewish War, he razed to the ground the entire city, except for these three towers. They were left to form a defensive position for the Roman Tenth Legion, which stayed in Judea as a garrison. (The Jewish historian Josephus claims that Titus left the towers intact as an offering 'to his own luck, which had proved to be his ally, and enabled him to overcome the city's impregnable defences.')

The large tower (**top centre in the aerial photograph**) is built on the lower parts of what remains of one of Herod's towers – probably Phasael. This stonework is one of the most extensive remains from Jesus' day still standing above ground in modern Jerusalem.

But for Christians, what is still more interesting is that Israeli archaeologists have discovered the remains of a massive stone platform inside the Citadel, and extending south of it into an Armenian garden. It seems that this platform formed the base of Herod's Palace, and the foundations of two large buildings, as well as coloured plaster fragments typical of wealthy residences, have been uncovered here.

The description of Jesus' trial in John's Gospel makes it clear that it took place outside the residence of Pontius Pilate, the Roman military governor. This probably indicates an outdoor podium with a large paved square, where a large audience could gather. Both the philosopher Philo, who lived at the time of Christ, and the Jewish historian Josephus, point out that Pilate lived in the former royal palace constructed by Herod the Great, so all the evidence goes to suggest that it was here, on the site of the present citadel, that Jesus was tried and sentenced by Pontius Pilate.

Inset: The towers built by Herod the Great; Phasael is in the foreground. This model of Jerusalem in the time of Christ is in the Holyland Hotel, Jerusalem.

Church of the Holy Sepulchre

'As evening approached, there came a rich man from Arimathea, named Joseph, who had himself become a disciple of Jesus. Going to Pilate, he asked for Jesus' body, and Pilate ordered that it be given to him. Joseph took the body, wrapped it in a clean linen cloth, and placed it in his own new tomb that he had cut out of the rock. He rolled a big stone in front of the entrance to the tomb and went away. Mary Magdalene and the other Mary were sitting there across from the tomb.'
Matthew 27:57–61

The question is whether this church is really built over the site of Jesus' tomb. In the nineteenth century the British soldier General Gordon queried its authenticity, pointing out that, against the Gospel record, the church stood inside the city wall. He favoured a site he found with a convincing-looking garden tomb, outside the city walls and near the Damascus Gate. What Gordon did not realize was that the Ottomans had expanded the city in the sixteenth century; in Jesus' time the site of the Church of the Holy Sepulchre would have been outside the city.

It is clear that, from early times, Christians believed this to be the site of Christ's death and burial. In 325, when the Empress Helena, mother of Constantine the Great, came to Jerusalem, she was shown the site, though the Romans had subsequently built a temple to Venus there. She demolished this so that a Christian monument could replace it. During the demolition, it is recorded that a tomb cut into the hill was uncovered.

The Constantinian church was built in the familiar basilica shape, with the rock-cut tomb at its centre. Although the original church was destroyed by the Persians in 614, it was later rebuilt on the same plan. This church, too, was destroyed, and the present building dates largely from the time of the Crusades. The Crusaders entered Jerusalem, the goal of their campaign, in 1099, and greatly enlarged the church, incorporating within its walls the supposed site of Golgotha, the place of crucifixion.

With its importance for all Christians, the church is today owned by six distinct religious communities: the Greek Orthodox church, the Roman Catholic church, the Armenian church, the Coptic church, the Syrian church and the Abyssinian church. Each community looks after specific parts of the building. The church has sustained extensive damage over the years, particularly as a result of a severe earthquake in 1927; since 1958 a major programme of restoration has been in progress.

Inset: Mourners at a Greek Orthodox funeral at the Church of the Holy Sepulchre.

Caesarea

'Three days after arriving in the province, Festus went up from Caesarea to Jerusalem, where the chief priests and Jewish leaders appeared before him and presented the charges against Paul. They urgently requested Festus, as a favour to them, to have Paul transferred to Jerusalem, for they were preparing an ambush to kill him along the way. Festus answered, "Paul is being held in Caesarea, and I myself am going there soon. Let some of your leaders come with me and press charges against the man there, if he has done anything wrong."'
Acts 25:1–5

The Phoenicians were the first to settle at Caesarea, and to build a harbour there. In 22 BC Herod the Great began the twelve-year task of rebuilding; his plans included a great semi-circular harbour, and a city with a theatre (**aerial photograph**), an amphitheatre and a temple to Augustus. The city, basically a gentile settlement, was named after the emperor Augustus Caesar, and offered the only good harbour on the Jewish coastline; Herod hoped to attract substantial trade.

When Judea became a Roman province, the Roman governors made Caesarea their seat of government. Among the governors based here was Pontius Pilate, and, later, Felix, who held Paul captive here for two years, until he appealed to Caesar. It was also at Caesarea that the apostle Peter met and baptized the Roman centurion Cornelius, provoking the great controversy in the early church over the entry of gentiles into the faith.

In AD 69 Vespasian was proclaimed Emperor at Caesarea, and raised the city to the status of a Roman colony. The earliest known church in Caesarea was built in the first century, and Eusebius, the earliest historian of the church, was probably born here, becoming the city's first bishop. When the Arabs captured the city, Caesarea lost its importance as a harbour. Later the Crusaders built their own settlement on the same site.

Although the site has still not been fully excavated, Caesarea has ample visible remains from both the Roman and Crusader periods. From the air, the quays built by Herod the Great can still clearly be seen under the surface of the Mediterranean. The harbour was vast, measuring some 1800 feet (500 metres) in length and 810 feet (270 metres) in width. Its quays had defensive towers and walls, which also provided living areas for sailors. Recent investigations have also revealed a huge tower at the harbour entrance, serving as a further defence, and possibly as a lighthouse too. Divers have also discovered the remains of wooden frames into which concrete had been poured during the construction of the harbour. The methods used seem to have been amazingly similar to those still in use today. In addition to the theatre, grain stores and parts of the harbour, the remains of the Roman aqueduct at Caesarea are also still clearly visible to today's visitor (**inset**).

Masada

This amazing fortress, built on a diamond-shaped site high above the shores of the Dead Sea, was one of King Herod's constructions. It has achieved immortal fame as the last stronghold of the Zealots, who held out here against the Roman army. In AD 73 they committed mass suicide rather than submit to Roman enslavement.

A small fort already existed on the flat-topped hill when Herod decided to build an impregnable stronghold here. He took six years to complete the fortress, equipping it with huge water cisterns, grain storerooms, barracks, arsenals and defensive towers, as well as a splendid palace. Thus it was equipped for the lengthiest siege.

The remains of the royal palace may be seen in the lower part of the aerial photograph, perched on the side of the mountain (**see inset**). Herod, always afraid of attack, decided this was the safest and most impregnable location for his own quarters. However, Herod died in Jericho at the age of seventy.

It was a few decades later, after the final Jewish rising against the Roman occupation, that the radical Zealots left Jerusalem and occupied Masada. After the destruction of Jerusalem in AD 70, it is estimated that about a thousand men, women and children were living in Masada.

In AD 72, the Roman Tenth Legion set about taking Masada. They surrounded it with a siege wall and with eight military camps, and proceeded to build a massive ramp to enable their troops to breach its defences. Masada fell eight months later.

However, when the Zealots realized that they could no longer hold out against the Romans, they decided that death was preferable to captivity. Suicide was prohibited to them. For this reason the men killed the women and children; then ten men, chosen by lot, slew the rest of the men; one man, again chosen by lot, killed the remaining nine, and finally ran on his own sword. 'When they discovered the numbers of the dead, the Romans did not rejoice at the enemy's downfall, but admired the noble decision and the unwavering defiance of death of so many people' (Josephus: *History of the Jewish War*).

Masada has today assumed an important symbolism for Jews. Israeli army recruits swear their oath of allegiance here, with the words: 'Masada must not fall again.'

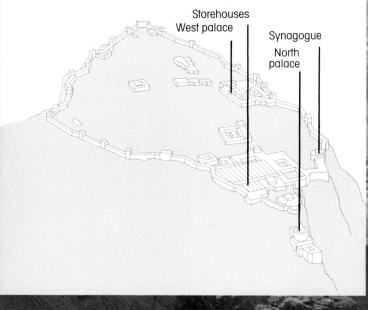

Storehouses
West palace
Synagogue
North palace

Mar Saba

Lying in the heart of the Judean mountains, but only eleven miles (eighteen kilometres) from the town of Bethlehem, the Greek Orthodox monastery of Mar Saba (St Sabas) is one of the most spectacular sights in Israel.

The present monastery, rebuilt by the Russians in 1838, is only the most recent of a number of buildings in this isolated location. In the early centuries of Christianity, hermits lived in the caves of the Kidron gorge, just west of the present monastery. In 492 a Cappadocian monk named Sabas founded the monastery, siting it opposite the cliff cave in which he first lived. Sabas was greatly revered; at the age of ninety he visited the Emperor Justinian to persuade him to rebuild the Church of the Holy Nativity in Bethlehem.

Later, after Persians and Arabs had destroyed the monastery and killed the monks, the community was restored and received its most famous member, John of Damascus, regarded as the greatest theologian of his age.

Only males may enter the monastery of Mar Saba. The small domed building in the middle of the monastery was built to house the body of Sabas. However, the Crusaders removed his remains, and when these were returned in 1965, they were placed in the main church. The bed of the river Kidron lies about 600 feet (180 metres) below.

Since women may not enter the monastery, a special tower was built to accommodate women guests. The tower, comprising a chapel and a dormitory, can be seen in the upper part of the main photograph, opposite the monastery itself.

Mar Saba ●

Avdat

Forty miles (64 kilometres) south of Beersheba, deep within the Negev desert, lie the ruins of the city of Avdat, with important remains dating from the Nabataean, Roman and Byzantine periods.

The first settlers here were the Nabataeans, who immigrated from north-west Arabia and founded the city around 312 BC, changing from a nomadic to a settled way of life. They built their capital city at Petra, famous for its rock-hewn buildings. The Nabataeans were great traders and depended on the commercial caravan routes for their prosperity. They built a series of towns along the route from Petra to Gaza, on the Mediterranean Sea, to protect the caravan route, and developed a sophisticated system of irrigation which allowed them to raise crops and provided them with drinking water.

At the end of the first century BC, Avdat became known as Obodas, after King Obodas II; 'Avdat' derives from his name. Obodas was buried here, and later came to be regarded as a god.

In AD 106 the Romans conquered the Nabataeans, and brought their territory into the empire as the province of Arabia Petraea. Although the new Roman road from Eilat to Damascus by-passed Avdat, the Romans later built a temple to Jupiter on the hill-top at Avdat, which helped restore its importance. During the reign of the Emperor Theodosius I (379–99), the Nabataeans were converted to Christianity, and later the Emperor Justinian (527–64) encouraged Christian monks to settle here. They reconstructed the Nabataean irrigation system, developed the agriculture, and built two new churches and a monastery on the site of the old temple of Jupiter. The larger of the two churches was dedicated to the fourth century Greek martyr St Theodoros; its arcaded basilica has been partially reconstructed by archaeologists (**aerial photograph**). It is not known to whom the other church was dedicated.

It was in this Byzantine period of its history that Avdat saw its greatest prosperity; but this was shortlived. The Persians captured the city in 614, and the Muslim Arabs in 634. Avdat gradually declined, and was finally abandoned; its advanced system of irrigation fell into disuse.

Inset: Bedouin girls on donkeys return from the desert water hole.

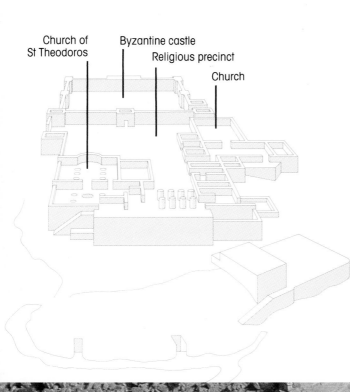

Church of St Theodoros   Byzantine castle   Religious precinct   Church

Page 64

INDEX